Blue and Green Things

Written by
Stephen Rickard

This shirt is blue.
It is not a green shirt.

This shirt is green.
It is not a blue shirt.

This pencil is blue.

This car is blue.

This car is green.
It is not a blue car.

This pencil is green.
It is not a blue pencil.

This bird is blue.
It is not a red bird.

This door is green.
It is not a red door.

This door is blue.
It is not a red door.

This bird is red.
It is a red bird!

Blue things

Green things